WORKING AT A
TV STATION

BY
GARY W. DAVIS

 **Children's Press**

A Division of Grolier Publishing
New York London Hong Kong Sydney
Danbury, Connecticut

Created and Developed by
The Learning Source

Designed by Josh Simons, SimonSays Design!

Photo Credits: Aerial Photography, Inc./Channel 4 Miami: 28; Channel 4 Miami: 15; Mark M. Lawrence/Channel 4 Miami: 4, 6 bottom right, 29 left; Tom & Therisa Stack/Tom Stack & Associates: Front Cover, 1-3, 6 left, 6 top right, 7-9, 11-13, 16-27; Bernard Wimmers/Channel 4 Miami: 5, 10, 14, 29 right, back cover.

Library of Congress Cataloging-in-Publication Data

Davis, Gary.
Working at a TV station / by Gary Davis.
    p.   cm. — (Working here)
Includes bibliographical references and index.
Summary: Describes the various kinds of career opportunities found at a television station.
   ISBN 0-516-20750-4 (lib. bdg.)   0-516-20378-9 (pbk.)
    1. Television—Vocational guidance—Juvenile literature.
[1. Television—Vocational guidance.   2. Vocational guidance.]
I.   `Title.   II.   Series.
PN1992.55.D33   1998
791.45'02'93—dc21

98-6412

CIP

AC

What comes to mind when you think of working at a TV station? If you are like most viewers, your first thought is of the people you see on the screen. In the television business, these **performers** are called the "**talent**."

In truth, though, there is little live talent at most TV stations. That's because most programs—action shows, comedies, even talk shows—are filmed or videotaped elsewhere. The finished shows are then broadcast from the station.

One kind of program, however, is almost always made at your local TV station—the news. At stations such as CBS4 in Miami, Florida, dozens of skilled workers put together live news programs that are seen morning, noon, and night.

News Director (right)

Who are these people? One very important person is the **news director**. She is in charge of all the news operations and decides how the stories will be broadcast.

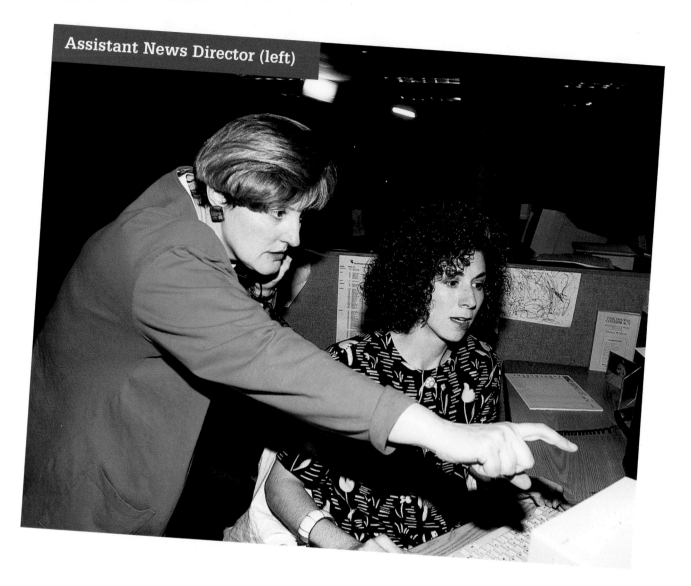

Assistant News Director (left)

The station also has an **assistant news director**. She does more, however, than just help the news director. The assistant news director makes schedules and supervises special reports and stories for the news shows.

Where do CBS4's stories come from? Some of the biggest stories come from large news-gathering organizations. These groups send in regular reports that can be shortened, edited, and read on the air (during a broadcast).

Other events come to the station by satellite.
Correspondents gather the news. These are people
who report from faraway places. Their stories are
transmitted to a communications satellite. It sends a
live report to satellite dishes on the ground called
earth stations.

From the satellite dishes, the story is sent to the TV station. There, the **satellite feed coordinator** uses special equipment to change the signals into TV programs.

Events that happen nearby are usually covered by **reporters** and **videographers**. They are on the scene of everything from fires to school events. Reporters do the research and interviews while videographers record everything on videotape.

News teams often work from vans. These vehicles take reporters, videographers, and their equipment to wherever the news is happening.

For live reports, an **electronic news gathering operator** creates TV signals. These signals go directly from the van to a receiver at the station, and then out to viewers.

Electronic News Gathering Receiver

When a van cannot get to a story, CBS4 sends out its helicopter, or chopper. With the help of a highly skilled **pilot**, a news crew is on the scene of an event in moments. Choppers also spot traffic problems on the area's roads and highways.

Not all reports come to the news room in a rush. Some reporters work weeks or even months for a story. These are **investigative reporters**. Like detectives, they carefully search for facts and information until they uncover the truth.

At the station, it is up to the **writers** and **editors** to turn all of these reports into a single news show. The most difficult job is making it all fit! There are so many stories to tell that each one usually is given only 30 seconds of air time.

Before the news is broadcast, a **videotape editor**
cuts, pastes, and rearranges the scenes by
computer. Everything must be in exactly the right
order, and nothing important can be left out.

A **videotape editor** also works on the tape to make sure that each reporter's voice is heard clearly. This includes mixing in background music and sound effects, too.

The diagrams, words, and other images
that appear on your TV screen are created by
graphic designers.

Most TV stations also have a weather center. Here, weather scientists, called **meteorologists,** study information from weather satellites. These facts are turned into forecasts that let viewers know what kind of weather to expect.

When the news is ready to be broadcast, it is time for the **news anchors** to go on the air. These are the men and women who actually read the news stories to viewers.

Many anchors write their own news stories. Then their words are typed into a prompter. During the broadcast, anchors read from the prompter screen in front of them. A **production assistant** operates the machine and guides the anchors along.

Once the show begins, the **TV director** takes over. She helps control the station's robotic cameras. She also works with the producer to make sure that everything fits into its time slot.

The director usually works in a control room. So does the **master control engineer**. His job is to make sure that every program and commercial airs at the right time.

In between the news stories come commercials.
TV stations make money from companies that pay
to have their ads on the air. **Account executives** who
sell this air time fill several offices at CBS4. So do
other executives who work at the station.

Watching over just about everything at CBS4 is the **general manager**. He is responsible for the operation of the entire station.

As everything comes together, the news is broadcast to viewers. Stations usually use tall towers to send TV signals. This one is over 1,000 feet (300 meters) tall, and can broadcast up to 100 miles (160 kilometers).

Thanks to the work of many people, these TV signals make their way to the homes of viewers like you and me. But perhaps you would like to help make the news, not just watch it. If so, maybe someday you will find yourself **working here** at a TV station.

Taking a Closer Look

Page 3

The control room has many monitors (TV sets). Each monitor shows scenes from a different camera either inside or outside the studio. The director uses these monitors when choosing which scene to put on the air.

Page 10

The very first communications satellite was launched into Earth's orbit in the 1960s. Ever since, satellites have relayed telephone and TV signals around the world.

Page 4

Television has two kinds of talent. There are the actors who play roles in comedies and dramas. Then there are the newscasters and talk show hosts who appear as themselves.

Page 12

Cameras used for broadcasting have viewfinders. With this tiny television screen to look at, the camera person is able to preview what you see on TV.

Page 6

To make sure their signals do not interfere with each other, stations in the same area transmit on different air waves, called frequencies. The group of frequencies over which one station broadcasts is known as a channel.

Page 13

The TV station's van is a mini control room. The van's electronic equipment is able to create live programs in locations away from the studio.

Page 15

In addition to filming news footage, helicopters also save lives. Sometimes they snatch people from burning skyscrapers and sinking ships. Other times helicopters land near accident scenes and rush injured people to hospitals.

Page 24

Once, the huge cameras inside a TV studio were operated by people. Today, most stations use robotic cameras.

Page 21

The name meteorologist comes from *Meteorologica*. This was the title of the book written by the Greek philosopher Aristotle almost 2,300 years ago. Even back then people were interested in weather conditions and observations.

Page 26

The price a station charges to run commercials is set by ratings. Ratings are an estimate of the number of viewers who tune in to each television program.

Page 22

Most TV productions use microphones that viewers don't see. One type, a boom microphone, is held above and in front of a performer. Another, called the lavalier, is a small "hidden" microphone attached to a performer's clothing.

Page 28

Television stations place their antennas on high buildings or towers so signals can reach as far as possible. TV signals usually can travel up to 150 miles (241 kilometers). When signals must travel further, other means of transmission are used.

Index